Motorcycling

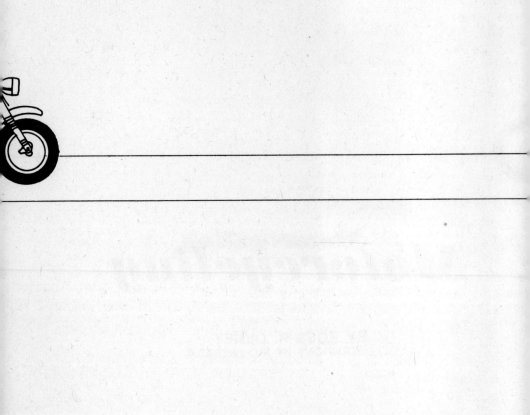

Motorcycling

BY ROSS R. OLNEY
ILLUSTRATIONS BY RIC ESTRADA

FRANKLIN WATTS | NEW YORK | LONDON

C1975 61 p. il.

Library of Congress Cataloging in Publication Data

Olney, Ross Robert, 1929-
    Motorcycling.

    (A Concise guide)
    SUMMARY: A guide to motorcycling includ-
ing motorcycling requirements by state, safety,
terminology, passing the license test, and book
and film bibliographies.
    Bibliography: p.
    1. Motorcycling. [1. Motorcycling] I. Title.
TL440.5.036   629.28'4'75   74-10720
    ISBN 0-531-02788-0

Contents

Motorcycling

How It
All Started

Paul Daimler was worried, though he was trying not to show it. Not that his father's ideas about engines weren't usually correct, but this time it was *Paul* who was going to do the testing.

Still, he had faith. He swung his leg over the unlikely looking contraption, glancing once again at his father for reassurance.

Gottlieb Daimler stepped forward with a match in his hand. He reached over and touched it to a Bunsen burner mounted at the side of Paul's vehicle, then he jerked a huge crank. With a swoosh and a flare of flame, the "engine" started banging away.

Never before had any type of internal combustion engine been mounted to wheels and made to carry itself and a passenger, but this was the year 1885. Old Gottlieb was sure it could be done, and he had invented the two-wheeled, bicycle-like framework to prove it. Then, since Paul was younger and no doubt quicker of reflex, he had asked his son to test the device.

The vehicle was an odd lash-up of wooden slats in a frame, fortified with pipes and topped by a saddle. It had two twenty-six-inch, iron-clad buggy wheels, one front and one rear, and then two more smaller wheels similar to the "helper" wheels on a child's bicycle. These latter wheels served as a form of landing gear, extending when the vehicle was sitting or (Daimler hoped) getting underway, then retracted by the man in the saddle. The wheels would not be needed during the "high speed" runs of the machine. These, Gottlieb hoped, would be in the breakneck range of seven miles per hour.

1

If the machine was strange, the engine was even more so. It had one single long, skinny cylinder, gas-fed through an amazing carburetor which metered the fuel to a combustion chamber *beside* the cylinder. The fire wandered about until it found its way to the proper spot to expand the gases and move the piston.

To ignite the fire there was a spark plug, right? Wrong! This was long before internal combustion engines used electricity for ignition. Remember the match and the burner? *That* was the ignition for Gottlieb Daimler's first-in-history motorcycle.

With one last fleeting look of concern at his father, Paul Daimler grasped the projecting "control rod" and shoved it forward. The crowd which had collected gasped and jumped back as the machine jerked, then jerked again. The control rod had tightened a belt around a pulley. At the same instant, Paul shoved down on the footboards and the two helper wheels snapped smartly in. The motorcycle was no Boeing 747, but it was as streamlined as Gottlieb could make it.

As the contraption bucked and jumped over the cobblestone streets of Cannstatt, Germany, Gottlieb stood back and smiled serenely, looking for all the world like an early-day Andy Granatelli. He'd had no doubt at all.

Meanwhile, Paul was holding on for dear life. The engine was turning at a fantastic 700 rpm's, and the machine was careening along at its maximum of Mach .01 (a full *seven miles per hour*).

However, a hill at the edge of town loomed ahead, and the machine slowed . . . and slowed . . . and *slowed*. But it didn't stop. Barely surmounting the rise (with the help of spectators who had been trotting along beside and fell in behind to push) the machine coasted down the other side and away. With hair streaming, proud of his father, waving very quickly to astonished pedestrians, Paul Daimler faded into the distance in a cloud of noise and smoke.

And so the world's first motorcycle jerked and popped its way into history. Daimler had proved his point, that an internal combustion engine could be freed from its connection to piped-in fuel and made to carry itself and a man.

But the great sport of motorcycling did not enter a boom period. Not yet. Daimler, having proved his point, shelved the whole idea and turned to other projects. It was many, many years before motorcycles entered their golden age.

Still, the light bike as we know it today isn't that much different from Daimler's invention. In appearance, the modern bike has two wheels, a saddle of sorts, and an engine below and between. In operation, both Daimler's original model and a modern bike engine are powered by vaporized fuel burning in a compression area. This burning of fuel still expands the air and pushes a piston in a cylinder,

which turns a crankshaft, which powers the bike (through Daimler's belt idea or through a chain on sprockets).

There, however, the similarity ends, for where Gottlieb's bike (which was, unfortunately, later destroyed in a warehouse fire) was ugly, uncomfortable, and probably quite hazardous to operate, the modern light motorcycle is sleek, easy to ride and handle, and as safe as the man in the saddle.

Looking back for one more moment, you might think that when Daimler turned his back on his invention he closed the door in the face of a persistent knock from opportunity. Perhaps, but Gottlieb Daimler was a sharp man. Though he ignored his toy, he went on to form the Daimler Motor Company, which is the forerunner of the Daimler-Benz Company, which is still world-famous today as the builder of the beautiful Mercedes-Benz automobile.

So we can leave old Gottlieb without sorrow, with a clear conscience and a fond smile. While he didn't make a nickel on the device that began today's big boom in small cycles, he didn't do too poorly for himself on other things.

The man who didn't do too poorly for himself in motorcycles was a shrewd Japanese inventor and market expert with a name you'll recognize instantly. This man envisioned a day when the motorcycle, which he found to be heavy, clumsy, and not really very much fun to ride, would become a vehicle for everybody. A vehicle light enough to handle, small enough to be relatively safe, and inexpensive enough for the workingman to own.

This inventor's name was Soichiro Honda.

Until Honda, most motorcycles were big, strong, heavily muscled vehicles that often could be handled only by big, strong, heavily muscled persons. The current police motorcycle is a good example of the "workhorse" type of motorcycle. Motorcycles of this type, which were almost all that were available, were sold from dark, dingy shops with motorcycle parts scattered about on greasy floors. They were often sold by huge men with dead cigars and scars and tattoos of knives through hearts and hula dancers on their arms. Only brave men entered these places of business, and then only if they perfectly understood the confusing motorcycle conversation and had cash on the barrelhead to pay.

Honda saw in the invention of Daimler, and even in the brute that it had become, the spark of a hobby and a sport which could sweep the world. So the Honda Motor Company was formed and it brought to the attention of Americans the lightweight motorcycle.

The sweep was on. Instantly the light bike caught the fancy of the Americans. It was an almost overnight sensation. Here was a classy little machine which was almost light enough for a man to carry, yet which could carry him over almost any terrain in relative comfort and safety. Here was a machine that was easy to start, easy to maintain, and inexpensive to buy and operate and insure. It would start with a quick kick, or a push of a button. Even youngsters could start it and ride it.

Honda made Daimler's motorcycle fortune, and he deserved it. Everybody wanted one of the new bikes. Thousands were sold, then hundreds of thousands. Today the Motorcycle Industry Council estimates that there are currently about 4.2 million street motorcycles in the United States. Add to this number about 1.3 million unregistered bikes and about 1 million mini-bikes and the total is close to 6.5 million — and the end of the boom is nowhere in sight.

Riding the Light Motorcycle

The Motorcycle Industry Council, made up of motorcycle manufacturers, suggests you *read* before you ride. Reading motorcycle material, and especially your owner's guide (the special manual for your
bike), will not make you an experienced, skilled rider. But you will
be amazed at what you can learn before you begin riding.

The fact is, motorcycle riding involves different skills than operating a four-wheel vehicle. Correctly learned, these skills can con-
siderably increase the safety of riding a motorcycle.

The design and engineering safety features built into a light bike
can make it safer than other vehicles, if these features are correctly
used. Consider the built-in advantages of a motorcycle:

• You have unlimited visibility on a motorcycle. The motorcycle
has no overhanging roof or closed-in, reflecting glass to obstruct
the view.

• The motorcycle has no "blind spot" to cut down on your field of
view.

• The motorcycle steers easily, usually by merely leaning, and
the controls on a modern light bike are simple and easy to reach
and operate.

• The braking system is positive, and very efficient. A two-wheeler
is capable of stopping within 70 to 90 percent of the distance required to stop the average automobile moving at the same speed.

• A motorcyclist's hands are always on the handlebars and he is
not distracted by other occupants, as is the case in an automobile.

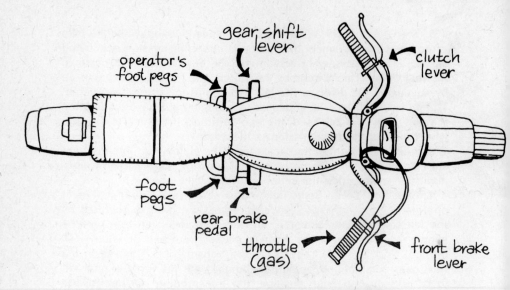

gear shift lever

clutch lever

operator's foot pegs

foot pegs

rear brake pedal

throttle (gas)

front brake lever

CONTROLS

Look at the diagram of the light motorcyle. Before you crawl on, learn the position, function, and limitations of each of these controls.

Then sit on the bike and practice operating each control (with the engine off) until you get the "feel" of them. You should be able to name, understand, and operate in minimum time each control on the bike *before* you start the engine. This is also a good practice for experienced riders when they try out a different bike. The guys at the motorcycle store get two or three chuckles every week as long-time riders dump a bike in the parking lot because they refused to "preflight" a model different from their own.

Let's look at the controls on the diagram:

1. *Front Brake Lever.* Light motorcycles have brakes on both front and rear wheels. Each brake is operated by a different lever. The front brake is applied by squeezing the lever by the right handlegrip toward the handlebar. On most bikes this will also operate the brake light. Remember, the front-wheel brake has more stopping power than the rear brake, and should be applied an instant *after* the rear brake as a general rule.

2. *Throttle.* Twisting the handlegrip toward you accelerates the engine, just as pressing the accelerator in a car makes the engine go faster. Do you see the logic of putting the brake lever and the throttle in the same hand? You won't be using both at the same time. As you turn the handlegrip away from you, engine speed is reduced. Most light bikes have a spring in the throttle which retards it when you release the grip, some do not.

3. *The Clutch Lever.* When the bike engine is idling, when the bike is not moving, or when the gears in the transmission are being shifted, it is necessary to disconnect the engine from the chain to the rear wheel. This is done by the clutch, and the clutch is activated by squeezing the lever by the left handlegrip toward the handlebar. When the clutch lever is squeezed, the engine is disengaged. When the clutch lever is released, the engine drives the chain to the rear wheel (unless the transmission is in neutral).

Some modern light motorcycles have the clutch built into the gear shifting mechanism. Operated by the left foot, shifting gears automatically engages the transmission at the right time.

4. *Gear Shift Lever.* Some light motorcycles have a gear shift lever operated by the right foot, while on others the lever is operated by the left foot. On our example, the more common left foot lever is shown. To shift gears, the lever is either depressed or lifted (with the toe). With each depress or lift, the transmission is moved to the next gear combination, without skipping. Until the lever is returned to its original horizontal position, the transmission will not go into the next gear. During gear changes, the clutch lever is squeezed, disengaging the engine from the rear wheel.

5. *Rear Brake Pedal.* On the right side (or sometimes the left side) a foot pedal is mounted to activate the rear brake. On our example, the more common right-side mounting is shown. Pressing on the pedal applies the rear brake, and activates the brake light on the rear fender of all street bikes.

6. *Lights.* Refer to the owner's manual for the position of the light switch and the low-high beam switch. These will usually be on the shell housing which encloses the light, or on the handlebar.

7. *Horn.* Usually a button within reach of the thumb on the handlebar. Refer to the owner's manual.

8. *Ignition Switch.* This key-type switch is located in different places, depending on the make of the bike. Refer to the manual for your bike.

9. *Starting Mechanism.* Modern bikes are started by the old faithful kick starter or by an ignition switch-operated electric starting motor. Refer to your owner's manual for locations.

The owner's manual will also give the location and operation of other features like battery, tool kit, crankcase oil-level checking device, passenger foot pegs, fork lock, and indicator lights. Locate each one of these on your own bike.

RIDING

After reading, the next step is riding.

Riding a light motorcycle is very easy to learn. Whether you are a beginner (be sure to tell the man at the bike store) or an experienced rider trying on a different bike, you will probably take your first ride in the parking lot. Wherever you ride, the area should be free of traffic and parked cars or other obstacles you might bump into. The area should be level and have a paved or very hard, flat surface.

You may feel a little foolish, but your instructor (who should be an *experienced* rider) will understand if you ask him to map out a ride for you, then to ride it himself first. Usually an instructor will order a short ride in the lowest gear so that you can become familiar with the "feel" of the bike before you try to operate certain controls. You can slow down with the brake and speed up with the throttle, without going very fast and without becoming involved with clutch and gear shifting.

Then, as you understand the bike, you can begin to shift up and down through the gears. During your low-speed riding, you will probably ride in a circle with the instructor trotting alongside to help. The whole thing might even remind you of Paul Daimler and the spectators trotting alongside him as he tested the world's first motorcycle, but this is still the best way to do it.

Brakes should be applied almost simultaneously, front and rear, with the rear slightly ahead of the front at normal speeds. Very soon shifting and brake operation will become second-nature and you will not have to think about it — though this might seem impossible to imagine when you first ride a light bike.

You will see skilled trials and moto-cross riders standing like jockeys, speedway riders raked forward with their knees flopping out, and a few "wild ones" left on the streets who lay back against a high seat rest. But the best way to ride is much like the way you sit in a car. Look at the illustration on the next page. Proper riding posture is important, not only for safety, but also for comfort — especially on a *long* trip.

9

The comfortable way to sit on your motorcycle is (1) with your back straight and not hunched, (2) with your arms slightly bent, (3) with your feet on the foot pegs, (4) leaning forward very slightly, and (5) with your knees hugging the fuel tank.

Sooner than you ever imagined you will be over the initial butter-flies-in-the-stomach feeling. You will be enjoying the ride instead of worrying about it. Then you can ride through simulated traffic conditions, to gain confidence. Set up some stop signs, parked cars, pedestrian objects, left and right turns, and other practice situations. Practice starting and stopping and firing up the engine.

And one other matter that new riders sometimes forget. Remem-

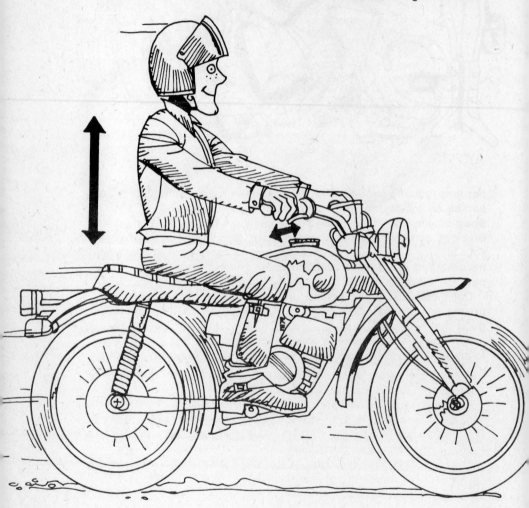

ber how to *park* your bike. Did you ever seen a bike which has been parked on a blacktop surface with a one-point kickstand? If it isn't down on one side, it may soon be, especially if the day is very warm. Blacktop softens, and the kickstand can melt into it. Always park your bike on a hard surface, and one that will *stay* hard. It might be necessary to use a block of wood under the kickstand, if you must park on blacktop.

Don't park too close behind an automobile, incidentally. If the driver can't see your bike in his rear-view mirror, chances are very good that he'll back over it.

Motorcycle theft is rather a common problem, and it is a good idea to always lock your motorcycle or to chain it to an immovable object.

Choosing a Bike and Insuring It

Who rides a motorcycle? Doesn't everybody?

Really, if you had to guess, who would you say? More males than females is correct, though the number of women motorcycle riders is increasing. Still, today, about 90 percent of all owners are men and boys.

Bike riders start early. By age thirteen or fourteen, boys (and some girls) are thinking of motorcycles. In fact, according to a recent Kawasaki survey, most riders enter the motorcycle market at from fourteen to sixteen years old, or after they have passed twenty-one. Older teen-agers either already own a bike, or are waiting until later to get one. More than half of all male motorcycle owners first became interested in bikes before they were sixteen. More than 36 percent of all female owners were first interested when they were younger than sixteen.

So motorcycling is a youthful idea, and getting more so every year. Fourteen percent of owners claim they were interested in bikes *before* age ten.

In selecting the correct first bike, ask yourself the following three questions:

1. How much do I want to pay or have to spend?

2. What kind of riding am I going to do?

3. What kind of motorcycle can I handle and control?

The answer to the first question can be found in your pocket. Only you can say how much money you have to spend on a bike. But whatever the amount, it is certainly an important consideration.

There are many different kinds of motorcycles. There are street cycles for on-road use, trail cycles for off-road use, and combinations of the two that attempt to have the best features of each, for both types of riding.

Street cycles are built to perform well in traffic and on paved streets. They have pavement-type tires, better brakes, lights, horns, and directional signals, and they have an engine and a transmission built to handle traffic speeds and conditions.

Trail cycles have special suspension systems built to handle rough ground. They have knobby tires with deep treads to dig into sand, mud, and soft dirt, and smaller brakes to reduce the chances of locking wheels on a loose surface. They have engines designed to produce more power at lower speeds. The trail cycle will not perform as efficiently in city or highway traffic, and it generally has no lights or other street-legal equipment.

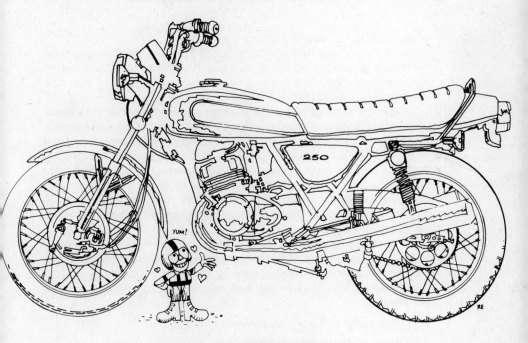

street bike

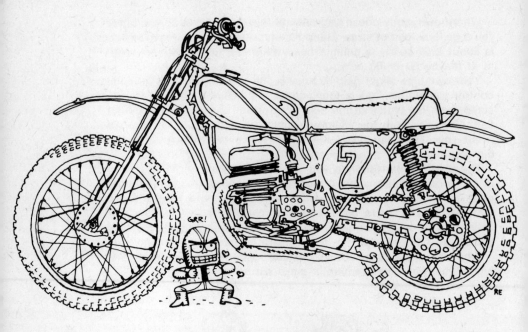

dirt bike

The compromise model is the effort of cycle builders to offer a bike which can go to the trail on the highway, then turn off into the dirt. Naturally certain sacrifices must be made at both ends to arrive at a good all-purpose bike. If you are not planning to be too demanding of either purpose (you don't plan to ride miles on the street every day, or you don't plan to spend every riding minute charging across the boonies) the compromise might be a good solution for both street and trail riding.

Motorcycles come in different sizes, and this always refers to the *engine's* size (measured in piston displacement in cubic centimeters, or *cc's*) and not the size or weight of the motorcycle itself. The more cc's of displacement, the more powerful the engine and the larger the engine. A 100 cc bike is smaller than a 250 cc bike.

Many motorcycle experts consider the following classes to be accurate:

Lightweights — up to 200 cc's
Mediumweights — from 200 to 400 cc's
Heavyweights — over 400 cc's

14

Where everybody doesn't agree with this exact spread, it will give you a general idea of sizes. The police-type motorcycle, for example, is about *1200* cc's — a definite heavyweight. Little mini-bikes weigh in at maybe 50 or 60 cc's.

Your own size might help to answer the third question. You can't control a machine that is too high or too heavy for you. Can you stand over the saddle of the bike in question and touch the ground flatfooted with both feet? Can you put both feet flat on the ground when you sit on the bike? If you can't, the machine may be too big for you.

There will be times when you will have to manhandle your bike in and around tight places. It must be light enough so that you can push it, and lift it onto its center stand. Take the bike you are considering and try to push it through a tight figure eight without losing balance or struggling too hard. If you can do it, the bike should be OK for you.

When buying a bike, always consider your own experience. The bigger, heavier bikes require a more expert rider.

combination street and trail bike

INSURANCE

Can you imagine how much it would cost you, or your parents, if you were to be involved in a serious accident on your motorcycle? If you are involved in an accident which is proven to be your fault, you could end up being required to pay for all the damages and all the medical expenses for *everybody*. This could cost thousands of dollars.

Then there is always the damage to your own bike to consider.

Motorcycle insurance is a valuable thing to have, and in many places it is legally required. That is, whether you are a car driver or a motorcycle rider, you may be required to show "financial responsibility" (the ability to pay for all damages in case you are judged to be at fault, by insurance or your own bank account). Usually any car insurance you have does not cover your motorcycle. You need a separate policy for two-wheelers, or a "rider" in your automobile policy covering bikes.

Bike insurance is not all that expensive, considering the protection it gives you. There are several insurance companies that specialize in this type of coverage, so what you must do is get quotes by telephone on rates from each one in your area. Find out just what their policy covers, and how much they charge. Then make your selection.

Insurance Requirements

As you price different insurance policies, be sure of what your state requires. There is no sense in getting something that won't be enough to cover legal requirements.

Remember also that insurance protects you for things other than accidents. Suppose you should forget to lock your bike, and somebody steals it? Or suppose it catches fire, or is tipped over and damaged by a vandal?

When you shop, keep these different types of insurance in mind. You will want most of these and certainly the first three (which, wouldn't you know, are the most expensive three):

• Liability coverage — pays for damage that you do to other people (personal injury) and other people's property (property damage).

• Collision coverage — pays for damage to your bike due to a collision, regardless of who is at fault.

• Comprehensive coverage — pays for damage to your bike due to anything other than a collision (fire, vandalism, falling objects, theft, storm, etc.).

• Uninsured motorist coverage — pays for damages when you have an accident caused by someone without insurance.

• Passenger coverage — pays the medical bills of anybody injured while riding with you on your bike.

• Medical payment coverage — pays your medical bills if you have an accident on your bike.

How to Pass the License Test and What the Police Watch for

In most states a special driver's license is required to operate two-wheelers on public streets and highways. This is the same as requiring special licenses to operate heavy trucks, buses, and other nonautomobiles. If you drive both a car and a motorcycle, you need two licenses, or one license with endorsements for each vehicle.

Let's take a look at the Department of Motor Vehicles rule book for information on motorcycle rider licensing. This is from one of the states where a special license is required and is typical of other states with such laws.

All motorcycles operated in such states must generally meet the same requirements as any other motor vehicle in that state. This includes safety equipment as well as emission-control features, and noise-abatement laws. If you bring a motorcycle into your state from somewhere else, be sure it meets legal requirements.

To obtain a license to drive a motorcycle in most states, you will be required to do the following:

1. Fill out a questionnaire telling about your physical condition.

2. Take an eye examination (though the wearing of glasses will not, of course, rule you out).

3. Take a regular written test on automobile driving rules.

4. Take an additional written test on motorcycle driving rules.

5. Take a skill and road test to demonstrate your ability to control and handle your bike.

Where most of the questions on the written tests will be much like the auto driver's questions (see *Driving: How To Get a License and Keep It* in this Concise Guide series), the handling test is different. Here is what you will generally be required to do before an experienced examiner:

1. Identify the starter, choke, clutch, throttle, gear shift, and brakes of your machine.

2. Start the machine and complete one or more figure-eight maneuvers (a sharp left-turning circle followed by a similar right-turning circle), without removing your feet from the footrests, wobbling, or falling.

3. Follow a straight line for at least fifty feet shifting gears as you go.

4. Make a sharp left or right turn at the end of the line and return to the starting point while shifting gears down.

5. End in a smooth stop.

Not difficult? Of course not, especially for a rider who has practiced until he has gained the basic skills. The idea of such tests is not to *prevent* you from cycling on the streets and highways, but to be sure that only the riders who have proven their basic skills will be out there with you.

Can you guess what the motorcycle policeman looks for when he sees you ride past on a motorcycle? Erratic riding and other violations of the law, yes, but *all* policemen watch for these things from *all* vehicles.

The motor officer is a skilled motorcycle rider. He is one of the very best bike riders on the road. He has been through tough, rugged training, his bike is huge and heavy, and he must ride many hours every day in all types of traffic and weather.

Former motor officer Charles Benoit, now retired from the crack Los Angeles Police Department motorcycle patrol, rode a huge motorcycle every day in a nightmare. Benoit's beat was the Los Angeles Freeway system, usually on the heavily traveled Ventura Freeway and one section of the infamous Hollywood Freeway.

"Bare feet," says Benoit. "If a motor officer sees a rider with bare feet, he knows that the rider has little knowledge of his bike. He is probably a new rider, and may not even have a license to ride a motorcycle."

No experienced rider would ride without boots, according to Benoit, not even "wild ones" who generally sneer at any protective clothing.

"You will get stopped and checked out almost every time by a motor officer if you are barefooted while riding.

"In fact, we always watched every rider for proper attire — leathers, helmet, boots," says Benoit. "If a bike rider doesn't know what to wear, he may not know the legal requirements either. We generally stop him to check safety equipment and condition of bike and license.

"Another thing a motor officer will watch for is a bike with no fenders. Whether or not the state has a law about this, it is a hazardous condition. The wind current will roll back debris and dust right into the rider's face if the bike doesn't have fenders."

To show what can happen to a bike rider no matter how skilled, Officer Benoit was very seriously injured in a crash on the Ventura Freeway. Not by another motorcycle, but by an automobile which swerved into him during a high-speed chase of a traffic felon. Benoit's heavy leathers were torn and scuffed almost through, his helmet was ground down almost to his head, and cracked. But the leathers could have been his skin, and the helmet his skull. He survived his injuries after months of convalescence.

Of course, you and I will never be chasing a criminal on a high-speed freeway, but Officer Benoit's case is a perfect illustration of the wisdom of wearing protective clothing.

Safe Clothing
and Safe Riding

Let's get directly to the point on this sticky matter of helmets. Whether or not you are wearing an approved helmet, if you run into an army tank head-on at full speed, you are going to get hurt — or worse. Wearing a helmet *guarantees* nothing at all. If we all admit that helmets are not *perfect,* than maybe we can face other facts with intelligence.

Here is the first fact.

If you do *not* wear a helmet while riding, you are *wrong.* It is that simple. No matter what some so-called experts say about whiplash (which still isn't as bad as a broken head), helmets are necessary and should be mandatory. No matter what others say about "limited vision," helmets can (and often *do*) save lives.

This is a fact. Where there is no documentation on injuries received *because of* a helmet, or because a rider's vision was limited by a helmet, there is overwhelming evidence of skulls which have been saved a bad bump by approved helmets.

Did you know that a modern crash helmet (or "brain bucket" to some) is a self-destructive device? That's right. The helmet is made to work *one time,* and no more. Of course that one time is all we ask of it, because then we are still alive to go and buy a new one. The lining material in modern helmets is made to "crush" under the severe pressure of a high-speed impact, slowing the head gradually so that no damage is done. Of course this all happens in an instant, but once it does the helmet has done its job. Racing drivers are very aware of this fact about helmets, but many bike riders are not.

Don't "test" your new helmet by banging against hard objects with your head. Such testing could begin to compress the lining, and besides, it looks silly.

Helmets are tested at the factory where they are built when technicians take random samples from the assembly line and destroy them. At every major helmet plant, they test according to requirements of the Snell Memorial Foundation and the Safety Helmet Council of America. The Snell Foundation was named after racing driver Pete Snell, who died in a crash when his helmet failed.

Such helmets are more expensive, but you are taking a chance with your head if you do not buy a helmet with either the Snell or the Safety Helmet Council sticker inside. Or, better yet, *both* stickers.

McHal and other companies test by dropping things on a helmet with an instrumented head inside. They jam hard, pointed objects at the helmet and then measure what happens to the head. They try to tear off the chin strap and they smash the helmet against flat, steel anvils. The electronic measurements tell whether or not the head was "injured."

Here are some official figures from the Congress of Automotive Safety, sponsored by the National Motor Vehicle Safety Advisory Council (in case you still have doubts about the worth of a helmet). This group analyzed more than seven thousand bike accidents from Michigan, which requires the wearing of helmets, and from Illinois, which does not.

Fewer than 1 percent of accident-involved cyclists wearing helmets received fatal head injuries, while 3.2 percent of the unhelmeted riders in accidents died from head injuries.

In Illinois 37 percent of the cyclists involved in accidents received head injuries; in Michigan 15.5 percent received head injuries. At speeds below 35 mph, unhelmeted riders are *seven times* more likely to die from head injuries than helmeted riders. Above 35 mph the ratio is about 3-1.

Still, in spite of these figures, the actual use of a helmet where it is not legally required is only about 28 percent. Hard to believe, but true.

Either goggles or some form of eye protection such as shatterproof glasses is essential to your safety. Not only can a flying insect or pebble damage your eyes, but such an object hitting your eyes can distract you just long enough to cause you to lose control. Never, never ride without eye protection.

Many bike riders wear gloves as a part of their protective equipment, especially if they are riding where brush or branches might hit their hands. In any case, gloves are a handy protection in the case of a lay-down, where the hands can get scuffed.

You are probably *not* one of those who thought that the old "black leather jacket and motorcycle boots" were to make a rider look *tough.* Many people think so, but the real reason these items were worn was to protect the rider. Imagine what happens when you rub sandpaper against wood, then visualize what happens when you rub skin against rough, hard pavement.

But not with a protective layer of leather. And feet and ankles are much less liable to injury or abrasion if boots are worn. Most riders today wear at least a long-sleeved garment when they are not wearing leather. A sport coat or sweater can help, and ankle-type boots under the pants look just as dressy as low shoes.

Every single safety-conscious motorcyclist does more than dress the part. He *rides* the part.

Have you ever watched a really good rider as he approaches his bike? Yes, he'll be dressed for safety, but he also *inspects* his motorcycle, *every single time* he begins a ride. Maybe not as thoroughly as a jet pilot walking around his plane, but the rider inspects all the same. He glances at the chain to look for sag, and he looks at the tires and rims. A quick squeeze of the clutch, throttle, and brake cables assures him that nothing has broken or drifted out of adjustment.

He checks his lights and horn, and he looks at fuel and oil levels before he starts the engine.

The safe rider is aware of certain riding problems of motorcycling. Some of these problems also apply to automobile driving as well, but they are especially important to the rider of a two-wheeler:

1. *Keep your distance.* Allow at least 50 feet between you and the vehicle in front if you are going 20 mph, 100 feet at 30 mph, and more than 300 feet at 50 mph. It *hurts* when you run into something that has stopped quickly in front of you.

2. *Stay alert.* Be prepared for vehicles pulling away from the curb, from a side street, or stopping quickly in front of you. Remember, many motorcycle accidents happen at intersections.

3. *Be seen.* "I never even saw him," is too many times the lament of an auto driver who has been involved in an accident with a bike rider. Turn on your lights day and night, and try to wear lighter-colored clothing.

4. *Use brakes correctly.* Be sure your brakes are in proper adjust-ment, then apply them in combination. Rear brake first, then almost

immediately the front brake. Apply brakes gently on slippery surfaces, and *before* you round a curve (not *in* the curve, which could
cause a dangerous skid).

5. *Don't drive where you can't see.* The only obstacle that can hurt
you is the one you didn't see in time, so be sure to see everything.
Don't pass on hills or curves.

6. *Use your mirrors.* With a mirror both right and left, you can see
everything behind you, especially before you change lanes. Some
modern helmets do cut down somewhat on side vision, so make up
for this loss with good mirrors, used constantly.

7. *Be especially careful making left turns.* Give yourself plenty of
room by moving to the left and signaling your intention well ahead
of your planned turn. Be sure oncoming traffic knows what you are
going to do as well as traffic to the rear.

8. *Be especially careful on slick surfaces.* You have two wheels,
not four. Automatically reduce your speed on a wet road, wet dirt,
or loose gravel. Remember that the center area of each traffic lane
is often heavily coated with oil which has built up from droppings

from automobiles. Ride to the right or left of this slick area, especially when it is wet. Also watch for oil slicks at places where cars stop, such as toll booths or parking lots.

9. *Concentrate.* The feeling of involvement between a man and his machine is never closer than between a rider and his motorcycle. But while you are mastering the basic skills of riding, try to develop a general "safety first" attitude that becomes a part of your involvement with your machine as you go out into traffic. This initial concentration toward attitude will pay off for as long as you ride.

10. *Never allow yourself to become over-confident.* As you gain riding skill, the temptation is to become at first completely confident in your ability, and finally *over* confident. It is then that an accident can happen. Keep just a small touch of fear in your riding. In almost every riding situation where there is a choice, you probably *could* have made it in fine shape, but the tiny touch of fear might often keep you from trying. An over-confident attitude will make you try every time, even in situations where you might *not* make it.

11. *Don't clown around on your bike.* Everybody loves a clown, and the rider who can make everybody else laugh will be popular indeed ... for as long as he, himself can ride. Showing off on the street is a mistake.

12. *There are no old, dumb bike riders.* Most available motorcycle accident statistics indicate two problem areas where motorcycle safety is concerned. These areas are *youth* and *inexperience.* And, of course, the two, together. While it is true that there are more young riders than old, the lower age brackets show higher accident rates *per mile* than the older age brackets. Also, the majority of motorcycle fatalities occur during the first few months of riding experience. This is true, in fact, with drivers of *all* types of vehicles (though, of course, the motorcyclist has less protection than an auto driver in an accident).

The key to motorcycle safety is to avoid the accident in the first place, the idea of the intelligent, well-trained rider.

There are old motorcycle riders, and there are dumb motorcycle riders ... but there are no old, dumb motorcycle riders.

Street and Highway Driving Tips

Bike riders must obey the traffic laws that regulate automobiles. And they have something else to think about. They must also be much more aware of the *surface* they are riding on. Motorcycles are vulnerable to every unusual surface. Even under normal conditions highways and streets have bumps, cracks, dips, and loose material. Add snow, rain, road debris, and other hazards, and you have a potential obstacle course for bike riders.

One of the most important rules in motorcycling is *Go around when you can.* But sometimes you cannot. The following tips might help when you must ride *over* a problem area: (And for every single problem area, keep in mind another primary rule of motorcyling: *Think* two *wheels, not four.)*

1. *Sand, mud, water puddles.* These will give you a problem in both steering and balance. Starting and stopping are also more difficult. Of course you will be especially aware when you are in these conditions, but you might also remember that more power than usual will help you control your bike.

2. *Tracks and metal surfaces.* Streetcar tracks, railroad tracks, and bridge expansion-joints should be crossed at a 90 degree angle whenever possible. Bike wheels can get caught if the angle is too wide. Reduce speed, and do not accelerate or brake when crossing the obstacle, if possible. Remember, a wet metal grating is probably one of the slickest surfaces you will ever encounter.

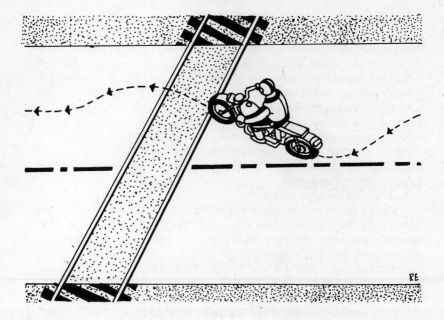

3. *Objects in the road.* The skilled bike rider is always scanning the road ahead, preparing to take evasive action in case he should come upon road debris. It is not unusual to find pavement chunks, bricks, rocks, lumber, boxes, and other litter in the road. One rider in California came upon a *coffin* laying in the middle of a freeway. He missed it . . . and it was empty — to answer both questions.

4. *Loose gravel.* You will sooner or later have to ride over gravel, dirt, rocks, and other loose debris. You'll find it like riding over marbles. These materials are *slippery,* a certain lay-down for a careless rider. Accelerate and brake slowly and carefully, keeping in mind that your stopping distance is much greater on these materials.

5. *Children and dogs.* In residential districts especially, children dart in front of bikes, and dogs seem to enjoy chasing motorcycles. Scan ahead and anticipate what a child will do. A child will almost always follow a bouncing ball, for example. Speed up to outdistance a dog, but don't try to kick at him. You'll only irritate the dog, and waste time getting away (as strong as the temptation might be to lay a boot in his chops).

6. *Automobile blind spot.* Thought you'd never have to worry about that on a bike, right? Now the problem becomes *his* not seeing *you* because of *his* blind spot. Avoid the rear on either side of every auto on the road. Remember Officer Benoit? He was struck by the rear of a car whose driver didn't see him.

7. *Intersections.* Motorcycles are safe, as safe as the man in the saddle, but the odds are that if an accident happens it will be at an intersection. And it will generally be between a motorcycle and a car — and we know who is going to lose *that* one, don't we?

You are sometimes easy *not* to see at an intersection, especially if trees, fences, parked cars, or other obstructions are present. The auto driver may not be looking for a motorcycle in the traffic stream. You may be nearer the curb, not in the direct line of traffic. Auto drivers sometimes have trouble judging the speed of a motorcycle.

Here's another motorcycle riding rule that works everywhere, but especially at intersections. Remember: *Always assume the other driver does not see you.*

And, wherever you ride:

Project a good image. Motorcyclists are special people. They are "different." They go their own way, they ride a special machine, they are generally more youthful, more outgoing, more daring. They have an "image." But the image can be hurt by a few bike riders who ride too fast, who ride without regard for the rights of others, and who pollute the air with noise. One removed muffler can turn the nonrider against all other riders, even the image-conscious ones. One lane-weaver can call attention to himself and away from dozens of safe riders.

Be proud of your sport, ride your bike safely, and with consideration for those still tied to four cumbersome wheels. Seeing you, they might give it a try, and your good image will have been responsible for still another conversion.

Off-Road and Trail Riding

One of the most popular bikes today is the off-road model. This is a motorcycle especially designed for rough riding on dirt, sand, rocks, and in backwoods areas (and often designed *only* for this type riding).

An interesting fact came out of a recent survey conducted by Kawasaki Motors, builders of a popular light motorcycle. In the northeast part of the United States and in the western part of the United States, *more than half* of all motorcycles sold are "dirt" bikes, or off-road models. And where men and boys far outnumber women and girls as motorcycle riders, *more than three quarters* of all female riders are dirt-bike riders. Riding off-road is easily the most popular form of the sport for girls.

But there is a problem. For a hundred years, people have been enjoying the back country, the trails, the remote desert, the high meadows, on foot and on horseback. Back-packing has been popular for nearly as long.

Then here we come, engine rumbling and exhaust fumes smelling. We are not, repeat *not,* very welcome. The first of ten tips for off-road riding, in fact, concerns courtesy. These tips come from the Motorcycle Industry Council:

1. *Use common courtesy at all times.* Other people along the trail generally do not interfere with our sport, so we should not interfere with theirs. Yet our motors can spook their horses, our noise can interrupt their peace and quiet, and our exhaust can spoil their clean air. The fact is, we *are* an intrusion.

We must give as much extra consideration as we can to others using the beauty of the back country. Yes, we have the right to be there as much as anybody else, even the right to make a nuisance of ourselves, but it isn't that difficult to avoid areas where nonriders are enjoying peace and quiet. As your own riding takes you farther and farther afield, you will become more experienced. You will learn where bike riders go, and where hikers and back-packers and horsemen go. You can plan your own riding to take into consideration the enjoyment of others.

2. *Never ride faster than you can see to stop.* Abroad in the land today are picnickers, campers, bird-watchers, hikers, and others. They are over the next rise and behind the tree ahead. Even if you know that the upcoming hill is a challenge and the jump over the

top a thrill, resist the temptation to go beyond your ability to stop quickly.

Around the next bend and coming your way might be a sportsman in a four-wheel drive truck or a dune buggy or even another bike rider. Can you imagine what might happen to you if a farmer has built a fence across where you plan to charge?

No matter where you ride, you will come up against natural and man-made obstacles. Sometimes where you can't see them until the very last minute. There is an old rather unpleasant joke about the man who survived a jump from an airplane even though his parachute didn't open. "It wasn't the fall that hurt," he said later, "it was the *sudden stop.*"

The same is true with trail riding. The sudden stop is the thing that hurts. Two boys were riding in an open field when they skidded into a recently strung cable. The passenger was not hurt, but the rider caught the cable in his throat. He survived, but it was months and major surgery before he could speak again. The cable had no apparent reason for being, but it was there — and he had hit it. Be prepared to stop and never go so fast that you can't stop within the distance you can see.

3. *Keep your muffler intact.* Trail bikes make noise, but they need not make more noise than necessary. Trail bikes can start fires in off-road areas, but they have equipment to prevent this from happening. Modern trail bikes are equipped with spark-arresting mufflers that prevent cylinder combustion from escaping from the exhaust pipe and also hold down the noise of ignition.

Removing or changing the stock muffler can affect not only the muffling ability of the unit, but also the spark-arresting ability. Exhaust cutouts, where the muffler is bypassed, are not only foolish but generally illegal. The same is true of removing the spark-arresting core from a muffler to "improve" the sound of the engine.

Point number one in this list suggests that we should be courteous, and extra noise on the trail only irritates other trail users. Worse yet, fire can be tragic. Leave your muffler alone. They knew what they were doing at the factory.

4. *Dress for the terrain.* Mother Nature, the one who clobbers the poor guy on TV for doing nothing more than mildly fooling her about margarine, can be *really* tough when she wants to be. This is especially true when you suddenly find yourself speeding down a trail ahead of your bike, with nothing under you but the seat of your pants.

You need a helmet even if the day is hot. You need good goggles even if they feel a little uncomfortable. Landing on your head or getting swiped across the eyes with a tree branch is not a pleasant prospect even if you are wearing protective equipment.

You need gloves on your hands, rugged boots on your feet, and tough leather or fabric on your body (waterproof if the day turns out to be wet, and cold-proof in the winter). Don't you believe those happy trail-bike ads where the guy is wearing a T-shirt and the girl a blouse as they charge off into a forest. They are really riding in their back yard. On the trail you must dress for the trail.

Due to the wind chill factor, motorcyclists are exposed to a condition known as hypothermia, a lowering of the body temperature. A drop of just a few degrees can cause a loss of concentration and slower reflexes, both quite dangerous when operating a motorcycle. The equivalent temperature on a 60° day for a rider traveling 60 mph is below freezing, so it is wise to dress a little warmer than what one might first consider appropriate.

5. *Keep off posted land and private property.* Unless you have permission from the owner, respect the right of others to keep people off what they own. There are people in the world who do not care for bike riders, and some who do not even allow hikers on their land.

Some of these people feel you might upset the balance of things in nature, hurt the ecology with your tires, your noise and your fumes. OK, it's their land. Ride elsewhere.

On the other hand, if you come outside the insulation of your helmet, goggles, and riding clothes and *talk* to people along the trail, you can do the sport a real service. Shut off your engine, take off your helmet, and pass the time of day. It is difficult to ignore a friendly approach, especially if you explain what you are doing and ask permission to carry on.

If friendliness doesn't win him over, write off the land, apologize for intruding, and ride back the way you came. Don't hurt the sport by acting hostile or arguing. When you are finished, he is still going to own the land, and by then he won't *ever* relent.

6. *Check your bike for reliability and safety.* Once again, don't tempt Mother Nature. A job you can do on your bike in the garage at home can be *fifty times* more difficult on the trail. Trails have a way of being dusty, or muddy, or rainy, or cold. Imagine trying to repair a broken chain on a cold, muddy, lonely trail as night approaches and you have stayed beyond your estimated time of arrival back home by several hours.

Before you hit the trail, check the oil level, fuel level, chain adjustment, controls, fork action, tire pressures, spoke tensions, all the major nuts and bolts, and the brake action. If you find something which needs attention, give it on the spot, not later on the trail.

Of course something might still break on the trail. Or a plug might foul. Carry along a minimum set of tools which should include a vice grip, a three-in-one screwdriver (with large and small blades and a phillips head), an adjustable wrench, and a good pocketknife. A spark-plug wrench is a must, and a chain breaker is also a tool you are not likely to find at a trailside farm house when you most need it. Will you need an allen wrench for your bike?

Spare parts? Absolutely. A spare spark plug or two can save a long walk, and a chain-repair kit can do the same. How about a spare gas line? Easy to carry and invaluable if you rip off the original or burn a hole in it. Another handy item to carry along is a roll of silver heating-duct tape. The stuff will repair almost anything, including ripped trousers. Many trail riders route a spare throttle-cable and a spare clutch-cable alongside the ones being used. Then if a cable goes awry, you merely hook up the spare (without worrying about difficult cable routing or parts removal on the trail).

A 10 foot length of nylon rope could come in handy — and matches in a waterproof container could be useful. In the desert, a canteen is a must.

7. *Ride with a buddy whenever possible.* Trails can be lonely places, especially when you break something which cannot be fixed or take a fall. The fact is trail riding does have its dangerous moments. Maybe that's a part of the challenge. Motorcycle trail riding is no different from other sports where an element of danger is present and where the "buddy" idea is stressed.

Sure, riding alone is dramatic and seems to satisfy a need for carefree abandon. But riding with a friend is smart and also fun. There are even times on the trail, in the desert in the summer or in the cold of winter, when Mother Nature can get angry enough to make the plight of a lone rider *desperate*.

8. *Avoid riding over vegetation or tilled ground*. Stay on the trail. The bike is made for trails, and this includes abandoned roads, beaten paths, old railroad rights-of-way, service roads, and even old cart tracks. Most trails are where men have traveled, and your bike can handle these without damage. When you leave the trail, you roar into places you should stay out of. You'll tear up ground, disturb the living habits of wildlife, crush vegetation, and risk collision with natural and animal barriers.

9. *Learn to read the trail*. Cross streams at rocky fords when possible. It's no fun to bang your knees on the bars as your front wheel drops into a deep hole in a stream bottom. Pick the places to cross streams where you can see the stream bed. When you see rocks in the trail, expect and prepare for more rocks. A sandy trail should prepare you to ride on more sand ahead.

If a wet log across the trail dumps you, remember how it happened, and hit the next one at a better angle. If a muddy rut lays you down, remember it and hit the next one with a little more power.

As you gain experience, you will learn to read the trail without effort. You will rarely be fooled, and your ride will be smoother and safer.

10. *Give horsemen and hikers the right-of-way*. It is unlikely that a hiker is going to walk on you, or even that a horse is going to step on you. But you can certainly damage a hiker or a rider (and yourself, too) by demanding the right-of-way. Be considerate. You'll get there much faster than they will anyhow, if that's important. Try to remember that we riders are the johnny-come-latelies. We must show them that we can live alongside them in harmony.

So bend with the breeze, and be polite to the walkers and the horsemen. Give them 51 percent, and sooner or later they will begin to realize that we aren't bad guys after all. Meanwhile, they are trying to legislate us out of places to ride — and in some areas they are succeeding.

For more information on trail riding, contact the motorcycle manufacturers listed at the end of this book, or write to the American Motorcycle Association (Westerville, Ohio) and ask for the booklet *The Trail Rider's Guide to the Environment*.

Competition

Many, many motorcycle riders feel that the ultimate fun of owning a bike comes with competition with other riders. Not necessarily for money (though many riders make an excellent living with prize money) but just for fun, as amateurs.

Sure, but only if you are an adult, you say. Wrong, says the American Motorcycle Association, the organization in charge of sport motorcycling and motorcycle competition in the United States since before 1920. The AMA has a branch for young competitors called the Y-AMA (for Youth Division). If you are seven years old, but not yet sixteen, you qualify for membership in Y-AMA. Over sixteen, of course, and you go into AMA.

The aim of the Youth Division of AMA is to enable young people to take an active part in motorcycling activities with other young people. The Y-AMA gives young people a chance to compete and encourages safe, responsible, and proper use of the motorcycle.

Here's an interesting fact you might pass on to your parents. National Safety Council findings, and many studies by private agencies, indicate that the more experience you have on a bike, the less your chance for an accident. As a young rider gains experience and handling skills, his chances of accident or injury continue to go down. The majority of accidents happen to riders in their first weeks of operation.

The Y-AMA activities provide a place for training, where beginning riders can learn how much fun a bike is while avoiding the hazards created by inexperience on the open road. You might want to become a member of an organized Y-AMA club, or form your own new club. Or, you can take part in all Y-AMA events by becoming an individual member not attached to any club. Contact the Y-AMA Youth Division Manager, Box 146, Westerville, Ohio 43081, for rule books, charter, and membership information.

Really small fry must be able to prove they can safely handle their machines before they can compete, but other than that most seven to fifteen year olds should meet all membership requirements whether or not they currently own a bike. There is no sex discrimination in Y-AMA, and the only size rule is a limit of 250 cc's on bikes.

Here are some of the exciting events held under the banner of Y-AMA for young amateur riders (prizes are trophies and points toward divisional and national championships):

1. *Dirt and short track races.* Dirt track races between bikes of the same size are run on specially prepared flat dirt tracks no greater than a quarter-mile around. Short track races are run on specially prepared flat dirt tracks no greater than 990 feet around.

2. *Hillclimb.* This is a series of trials against time or distance, on a hill specially prepared for climbing. A hillclimb attempt ends when the forward progress of a bike stops with the rider astride the vehicle. The hill is usually steep, and well chewed-up by the wheels of previous bikes. The action is *wild!*

3. *Scrambles.* This event is conducted on an unpaved course or field specially prepared for the meet. Designed to test the rider's skill rather than the speed of the bike, the course is irregular so that right and left turns as well as gear-changing hills are included. Jumps are permissible in this event.

4. *Cross-country and hare-and-hound races.* Contests over cross-country courses, where rider ability is the determining factor. These courses include dirt roads, trails, footpaths, up and down hills, and other terrain as long as it is safe and possible to negotiate. Checkpoints may be established to record the progress of riders, who must check in and out. Often there are follow-up crews of adults in trucks to pick up riders and bikes with mechanical failures, since these events are tough on rider and bike.

5. *Moto-cross.* One of the most popular of the motorcycle races, especially among adult professional riders, this event is conducted on a closed, rough, and rugged course. Turns and jumps must be negotiated, as well as rough, rutted paths, mudholes, and slippery areas. You may look like a mudball yourself after a moto, but this is *exciting* riding.

The trick in moto-cross is to stay up long enough to beat everybody else to the finish. Since the course for moto-cross must be a half-mile long and no more than one and a half miles, everything happens within sight of the pits and (perhaps unfortunately) parents — among whom this is not the most popular event.

As a member of Y-AMA you can also participate in *enduros; ice races; dirt drag races;* and *observed, Scottish,* and *pavement trials* (where *superb* riding skill is necessary to win, but where speed counts for very little).

One of the nice things about competing with Y-AMA is that since your own bike must meet certain safety and performance requirements, you know that everybody else's must meet the same. And you, yourself, must meet safety standards by wearing protective helmets and other apparel. Full leathers are not generally required (though they are recommended) but you must wear boots, protective clothing, gloves, and a steel skid shoe (in certain events).

Prospective "wild ones," however, need not apply. The Y-AMA is serious about both a pledge and a code of conduct. Here is what you must agree to abide by, and sign:

THE PLEDGE OF THE YOUTH DIVISION

As a member of the Youth Division of the American Motorcycle Association, I pledge to operate my motorcycle in a safe and responsible manner. I pledge to use it properly and quietly with appropriate courtesy to the individuals around me. I will strive to foster safe operating habits in myself, and I will always try to impart my knowledge of safe operation to my fellow riders.

CODE OF CONDUCT

1. At all times I will conduct myself in a manner reflecting credit on my club, my community, the American Motorcycle Association and the sport of motorcycling.

2. I will ride in a safe manner, obeying all local and state traffic regulations and all rules of the Youth Division of the American Motorcycle Association.

3. I will keep my machine clean and in proper tune, replacing promptly all worn or damaged parts.

4. While participating in Y-AMA activities, I will demonstrate the highest principles of sportsmanship, obeying promptly and courteously all instructions of designated officials.

5. I will take an active part in all activities of my Youth Division Club, realizing that participation and loyalty are the keys to club success.

6. I will refrain from the use of alcohol and narcotics and will not associate with those who use these substances.

7. I will do all in my power to promote the good aspects of motorcycling as expressed in the American Motorcycle Association Youth Division Rulebook.

Motorcycle Classifications

Motorcycles fall into certain broad classifications, though many types are very often ridden in areas other than that in which they are classed. A mini-bike, for example, though designed for off-road use, can just as easily, with the addition of lights and horn, be ridden to the grocery store.

MINI-BIKE. Generally one cylinder, 75 cc or less, small wheels, and depending on accessories, designed for on or off-road use.

STREET MODEL. A motorcycle of any size equipped with accessories to make it legal for riding on streets or highways.

TRAIL BIKE. A motorcycle of any size equipped with accessories (or the lack of them) to make it convenient to ride on trails. Often called an "off-road" model.

TOURING BIKE. A somewhat larger street-legal model for longer rides at higher speeds. Rider comfort in the form of more power, better saddle, comfort accessories, is a greater factor.

MOTO–CROSS MODEL. A bike designed with rugged strength and low range power specifically for tough competition. Not legal on the street.

ROAD RACER. A bike of 350 cc or more designed for high speed road racing, generally equipped with a streamlining fairing to cut down on wind resistance for greater speed. Not legal on the street without additional accessories.

DIRT TRACK RACER. A motorcycle designed for dirt track racing. This is a ruggedly built, high powered bike with one distinctive feature . . . it has no brakes.

DUAL PURPOSE BIKE. Sometimes called a Street/Trail Bike, this model has certain features of the street bike to make it street legal (lights, horn, etc.) and certain features of the trail bike to make it fun on dirt (good low range power, knobby tires, high exhaust, etc.). This is one of the most popular motorcycles of all, and comes in a wide variety of engine sizes.

There are other models designed specifically for certain purposes, such as a side-hacker (with a flat sidecar) for racing, a "speedway" bike of lower power and great strength for racing on a very short dirt circle, and different types of trials bikes for competitions where skill is the deciding factor and not speed. There are also large, powerful, high speed police models, and motorcycles which have been redesigned for jumping and other stunt work.

Motorcycle Terminology

AMA. American Motorcycle Association, national sanctioning organization.

AMDRA. American Drag Racing Association.

BAJA. Lower California, Mexico, annual 500, 1,000 mi. endurance runs.

BERM. A pile of dirt formed on the outside of a turn on a dirt track.

BIKE. Slang for motorcycle.

BINDERS. Brakes.

BLACK FLAG. Disqualifies individual rider in all types of racing (most often used where bike is hazarding other riders).

BLUE FLAG. Rider trying to pass.

BONNEVILLE. Salt flats, speed record attempts.

BOONIES. An isolated riding area.

BORE. Cylinder diameter.

BORED. An engine increased in size by enlarging cylinders and pistons.

C.D.I. Capacitor Discharge Ignition.

CHECKERED FLAG. Black and white, end of race.

COLORS. Term signifying racing colors such as Kawasaki team riders in green and white leathers.

CONTINGENCY AWARD. Motorcycle, parts, and accessory manufacturers offer prizes in addition to purse money, for winning or placing riders using their product.

ENDURO. The name given to dirt and street motorcycles, and racing with varying times and speeds.

EXPANSION CHAMBER. A specially designed exhaust pipe for two-stroke engines.

EXPERT CLASS. The highest division of AMA professional motorcycle racing.

FAIRING. A fiberglass shell used on roadracing bikes for streamlining purposes. Can add several MPH to the top speed.

F.I.M. Fédération Internationale Motorcycliste, international sanctioning organization.

FLAT TRACK. Round or oval shaped dirt tracks one-quarter to one mile around.

FORK BOOTS. A rubber fitting used to keep dirt out of front forks.

FORK BRACE. A heavy aluminum brace designed to keep forks in line under hard use.

FRAME. The basic assembly of a motorcycle without wheels, engine or fairing.

FUELER. As in car racing, a motorcycle using esoteric mixtures of fuel — i.e. "nitro" — to achieve greater speeds in drag racing.

GET OFF. An abrupt unplanned departure from the seat of a motorcycle.

HARE & HOUND. Desert race of 60 to 100 miles where several hundred riders (hounds) give chase to one rider (hare).

HEAT RACE. A race used to choose finalists for a main event.

I.S.D.T. International Six Day Trials, annual international enduro — "Olympics of Motorcycling."

JUNIOR CLASS. Middle division racer, has not accumulated enough points to move into expert division.

KIDNEY BELT. Worn by many professionals to prevent internal injuries caused by vibration or jarring.

KNOBBIES. Special tire with large rubber cleats provides excellent traction on dirt.

LEATHERS. A protective racing suit made of leather.

MIC. Motorcycle Industry Council.

MOTO–CROSS. A marked course consisting of treacherous natural and man-made obstacles.

NOVICE CLASS. Beginning division of motorcycling competition.

ON THE PIPE. An engine running at peak power.

OVERSQUARE. An engine with its bore larger than its stroke.

PEAKY. An engine with a limited range of power.

PILLION. Small seat on rear fender of racing machine.

PINGING. Engine clatter caused by preignition or low octane fuel.

POWER BAND. Efficiency range of engine.

RED LINE. Point of maximum engine efficiency.

RIGID FRAME. A bike without rear suspension.

RIM LOCK. Keeps tire from rotating on rim.

RPM. Revolutions Per Minute of engine crankshaft.

SCRAMBLES. Planned course racing over rough terrain.

SEIZE. An engine lock up.

SHORT TRACK. Closed dirt course of less than a half mile.

SHROUDS. Dust protectors for levers.

SHUT THE DOOR. To cut someone off.

SIDEHACK. Motorcycle side car used in two-man team sidecar racing, a European sport gaining popularity in America.

SKID PLATE. Protective metal plate under the engine to prevent damage from rocks in off-road riding.

SKINS. Tires or leather clothing.

STINGER. Rear portion of expansion chamber.

STOCK BIKE. A motorcycle with minimal modifications. May or may not be street legal. Most often found in drag racing and enduros.

STREET BIKE. Usually a street-legal motorcycle with *no* modifications.

STROKE. Distance piston travels.

SWING ARM. Rear suspension arm.

THUMPER. Single cylinder four-stroke motorcycle.

TICKLE. The deliberate priming of an engine to facilitate starting.

TRIALS. Competition with emphasis on skill over rough terrain.

TRIPLE CLAMP. Secures forks to pivot.

T.T. (Steeplechase). Closed dirt track course with several right and left turns and a jump.

TUNER. Usually the chief mechanic for a racer.

TWO-STROKE. A motorcycle which has a power stroke with each revolution of the engine.

UNDERSQUARE. Engine with stroke larger than bore.

WHITE FLAG. One lap to finish.

WHITE FLAG w/RED CROSS. Ambulance needed.

WHOOP-DE-DOOS. A continuous series of dips and rises in rapid succession.

WRENCH. A mechanic or pit crew member.

YELLOW FLAG. Danger on track.

YELLOW FLAG WITH RED STRIPES. Oil on track.

Courtesy
KAWASAKI MOTORS CORP.

Films About Motorcycling

"Stone Age Rules of the Road". 16mm, sound, color. A basic driver education film. Produced in cooperation with the National Safety Council. Available on free loan basis from the Motorcycle Industry Council, 1001 Connecticut Avenue, N.W., Washington, D.C., 20036.

*"Critical Hours". 16mm, color, sound. Available from local BSA dealers or Public Relations Department, BSA Motorcycle Corp., P.O. Box 402, Duarte, CA 91010.

*"The Invisible Circle". 16 mm, color, sound. Available from local Honda dealers or Public Relations Department, American Honda Motor Co., 100 West Alondra Blvd., Gardena, CA 90247.

*"Background to the Motorcycle". "Natural Forces and the Motorcycle". "Operation of the Motorcycle". 16mm, color, sound. 40 min. (3-13$^{1}/_{3}$ min. segments). Available from local Honda dealers or American Honda Motor Co.

"The Swinging World of Sportcycles". Shows the fun and wholesomeness of sportcycling, and in doing so, incorporates some material on safety. Produced by Yamaha International Corp. Available from local Yamaha dealers, or Public Relations Director, Yamaha International Corp., 6600 Orange Thorpe, Buena Park, CA 90620.

*"Cycle Logic, Cycle Safety". 16mm, color, sound. Available from USAF Audio Visual Center (AVVCC) Norton AFB, CA 92409. Training Film No. TF-5990.

*Available on short-term free-loan from Technical Reference Division (N48-52), National Highway Traffic Safety Administration, U.S. Department of Transportation, Washington, D.C. 20591

"*Stay Alert, Stay Alive*". 16mm, color, sound. 20 min. training film for police motorcyclists. Stresses defensive driving practices. Sponsored by the CA Highway Patrol. Available on free loan to police departments within California. May be purchased for $250.00 from United Research and Training, Inc., 5525 Wilshire Blvd., Los Angeles, CA 90036.

"*Basic Rider Training Program*". 22 min., color, 1970. Available for free loan from local Yamaha dealers or Public Relations Director, Yamaha International Corp. 6600 Orange Thorpe, Buena Park, CA 90620.

"*The Trail Bike Experience*". 28 minutes 16mm, sound, color documenting the joys of trail riding and emphasizing the good neighbor aspects of conduct on the trails. Available on a five day free-loan basis from Motorcycle Industry Council.

"*Behind the Handlebars*". 16mm, each approximately 40 minutes, color/sound, available for purchase or on a free-loan basis. This four-part motorcycle simulator film series is a first in the motorcycle industry. Each film is designed to show how actual riding is done "behind the handlebars." The series includes: 1 "The Residential Ride;" 2. "Meeting Traffic;" 3. "Advanced Traffic;" and 4. "Special Conditions". These films can be used in conjunction with simulators in motorcycle rider education and safety programs. Available from American Honda.

"*Attitude in Motion*". 16mm, approximately 35 minutes, color and sound. Develops the need to assert the proper attitude while riding a two-wheel motor vehicle. The attitudes of safety and defensive riding are incorporated in the film, as well as the proper outlook on riding in general. The film depicts how the Long Beach (California) Police Department started a motorcycle safety program within their community. Available for purchase or free loan from American Honda.

"*Safety Rider*". 16mm, 12 minutes, color, brings to the audience salient points of safety to cyclist and car driver alike in an entertaining manner. Available for purchase $180.00, preview showing $20.00. International Association of Chiefs of Police, Inc., 11 Firstfield Road, Gaithersburg, MD 20760.

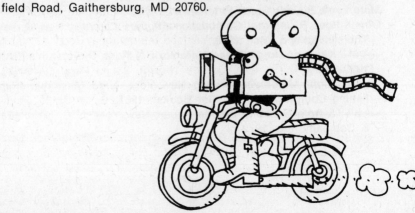

Books About Motorcycling

Behme, Robert. *Motorcycle and Trail Bike Book* New York, N.Y.: Pyramid Communications, Inc., 1971.

Clymer, C. F. *A Treasury of Motorcycles of the World* New York, N.Y.: McGraw-Hill Book Company, 1965.

Griffin, Al. *Motorcycles: A Buyer's and Rider's Guide* Chicago, Illinois: Henry Regnery Company, 1972.

Guide to Safe Motorcycling American Automobile Association, 1971.

Hailwood & Walker. *The Art of Motorcycle Racing* Land, Cassell, 1966.

Halsey, Maxwell and Richard Kaywood. *Let's Drive Right* Glenville, Illinois: Scott, Foresman & Company, 1968.

Jones, T. F. *Enduro* Radnor, Pennsylvania: Chilton Book Company, 1970.

King, Max. *Trials Riding* London: Temple Press, 1970.

Motorcycle Buyer's Guide Petersen Publishing Company, 1970.

Olney, Ross R. *Internal Combustion Engines* Camden, New Jersey: Thomas Nelson, Inc., 1969.

————. *Kings of Motor Speed* New York, N.Y.: G. P. Putnam's Sons, 1970.

————. *Light Motorcycle Riding* New York, N.Y.: Macmillan Publishing Company, Inc. (Collier Books), 1967.

————. *Simple Gasoline Engine Repair* New York, N.Y.: Doubleday & Company, Inc. 1972.

Richmond, Doug. *All About Minibikes* Tucson, Arizona: H. P. Books, 1970.

Ritch, O Cee. *Chilton's Motorcycle Troubleshooting Guides* Radnor, Pennsylvania: Chilton Book Company, Annual.

Sanford, Bob. *Riding the Dirt* Newport Beach, California: Bond, Parkhurst & Bond, Inc., 1972.

Wallach, Theresa. *Easy Motorcycle Riding* New York, N.Y.: Bantam Books, Inc., 1971.

Watson, Jack. *How to Buy a Used Motorcycle* New York, N.Y.: Barnard, 1971.

Motorcycle Requirements by State

STATE	Special Driver License	Safety Helmet	Eye Protect.	Passenger Seat	Passenger Foot Rests	Mirror Required	Safety Inspection At time of Reg.	Safety Inspection Periodically	Lights on all times	Handlebar 15" Ht. Limit	Riding Prohibited Two Abreast	Riding Prohibited Between Lanes	Riding Prohibited Side Saddle
ALABAMA	X-A	X		X	X								X
ALASKA	X-B	X	X	X	X	X				X		X	X
ARIZONA	X	X	X	X	X	X				X	X	X	X
ARKANSAS		X	X	X	X		X	X-C	X				
CALIFORNIA	X			X	X	X		X-C	X-D	X-E		X	X
COLORADO	X	X	X			X	X	X				X	X
CONNECTICUT	X	X	X	X	X	X	X	X-C	X	X	X	X	X
DELAWARE	X-F	X	X	X	X	X	X	X		X		X	X
FLORIDA		X	X	X	X	X	X	X	X	X		X	X
GEORGIA	X	X	X	X	X	X	X	X	X	X		X	X
HAWAII	X	X	X	X	X	X	X	X		X		X	X
IDAHO		X		X	X		X	X		X		X	X
ILLINOIS	X		X	X	X	X			X	X	X	X	X
INDIANA		X	X	X	X	X	X	X	X	X		X	X
IOWA				X	X	X	X-G			X		X	X
KANSAS		X	X	X	X	X	X			X-E		X	X
KENTUCKY	X	X	X	X	X	X	X	X				X	X
LOUISIANA	X	X	X	X	X	X	X	X		X		X	X
MAINE	X	X		X	X	X	X			X		X	X
MARYLAND	X	X	X	X	X	X		X		X	X	X	X
MASSACHUSETTS	X	X		X	X	X	X			X	X	X	X
MICHIGAN	X	X	X-H			X		X-C		X-E		X	X
MINNESOTA	X	X		X		X		X-C		X-E		X	X
MISSISSIPPI						X		X					
MISSOURI	X	X						X		X			
MONTANA	X			X	X		X	X	X				X
NEBRASKA		X		X	X		X	X				X	X

50

NEVADA	X	X	X	X	X	X	X		X				X
NEW HAMPSHIRE	X	X	X	X	X	X	X		X		X		X
NEW JERSEY	X	X	X	X	X	X			X				X
NEW MEXICO	X-I	X	X	X	X	X	X		X		X		X
NEW YORK	X	X	X	X	X	X	X	X	X	X	X	X	X
NORTH CAROLINA	X		X	X	X	X			X				
NORTH DAKOTA	X	X	X	X	X	X			X			X	X
OHIO	X	X	X	X	X				X-L	X	X	X	X
OKLAHOMA	X-J	X-K	X	X	X	X			X-L	X	X	X	X
OREGON	X	X	X	X		X-C			X			X	X
PENNSYLVANIA	X	X	X	X	X	X			X			X	X
RHODE ISLAND	X	X	X	X	X	X			X			X	X
SOUTH CAROLINA	X	X	X	X	X	X		X	X		X	X	X
SOUTH DAKOTA	X	X	X	X	X	X			X	X		X	X
TENNESSEE	X	X	X	X	X	X			X			X	X
TEXAS	X	X	X	X	X	X			X			X	X
UTAH	X-M	X-M	X	X	X	X	X-E		X	X	X	X	X
VERMONT	X	X	X	X	X	X		X	X			X	X
VIRGINIA	X	X	X	X	X-N	X			X	X		X	X
WASHINGTON	X	X	X	X-C	X-C	X			X		X	X	X
WEST VIRGINIA	X		X	X	X	X			X			X	X
WISCONSIN	X	X	X	X-C	X-C	X			X		X	X	X
WYOMING	X	X	X	X	X	X			X		X	X	X
DIST. OF. COL.	X	X	X	X	X	X		X	X			X	X

A. Required if under 16 yrs.
B. Required after July 1, 1973
C. Random vehicle inspection
D. Required after Jan. 1, 1975
E. Handgrips below shoulder height
F. Endorsement on license
G. First registration after sale
H. Required for speeds over 35 mph
I. Operators & passengers under 18
J. 14-16 yrs. old restricted to hrs., speed & horsepower
K. Operators & passengers under 21
L. Height limit 12 inches
M. On roads with speed limits over 35 mph
N. At time of special endorsement on license

Information Sources on the Motorcycle Industry

ORGANIZATION AND ADDRESS	NAME	TITLE
Motorcycle Industry Council 1001 Connecticut Ave., NW Suite 732 Washington, D.C. 20036 Telephone 202-223-9158	James B. Potter, Jr. Pat Young Bill Kennedy (Rex Chainbelt)	Exec. Director Public Relations President
Motorcycle Industry Council Safety & Education Foundation 1001 Connecticut Ave., NW Suite 701 Washington, D.C. 20036 Telephone 202-293-3050	Dr. Charles H. Hartman James Carfield Les White (American Honda)	Exec. Director Public Relations President
Cycle Magazine One Park Ave. New York, N. Y. 10016 Telephone 212-679-7200	P. Thomas Sargent Cook Neilson	Publisher Editor
Cycle World Parkhurst Pub. Co. 1499 Monrovia Ave. P.O. Box 1757 Newport Beach, Calif. 92663 Telephone 714-646-4455	Joseph C. Parkhurst Ivan Wagar	Publisher Editor
Motorcyclist Petersen Pub. Co. 8490 Sunset Blvd. Los Angeles, Calif. 90069 Telephone 213-657-5100	Peter Nicolaysen Bob Greene	Publisher Editor

54

Kawasaki Motors
1062 McGaw Ave.
Santa Ana, Calif. 92705
Telephone 714-540-9980

Tom LeCog — Asst. Public Relations Mgr.

American Honda
100 W. Alondia
Gardena, Calif. 50247
Telephone 213-327-8280

Iwao Matsuoka — Public Relations Mgr.

Yamaha International
P.O. Box 6600
Buena Park, Calif. 90620
Telephone 714-522-9011

John Rinek — Public Relations Mgr.

Harley Davidson
3700 W. Juneau
Milwaukee, Wisc. 53208
Telephone 414-342-4680

Thomas Swain — Public Relations Mgr.

Triumph, Inc.
80 Pompton Ave.
Verona, N. J. 07044
Telephone 201-239-8120

Feliz A. Kalinski — President

Champion Spark Plug Co.
P.O. Box 910
Toledo, Ohio 43601
Telephone 419-536-3711

Jerry Grant — Public Relations Dept.

55

Webco, Inc. (Accessories)
218 Main St.
Venice, Calif. 90291
Telephone 213-870-7758
or 399-7724

T. N. Heininger   President

AESI
Automotive Environmental Systems, Inc.
7300 Bolsa Ave.
Westminster, Calif. 92683
Telephone 714-897-0333

M. Van Loan   Chairman &
                                   Secretary-Treas.

Trippe, Cox Associates, Inc.
Suite 17B
19531 Airport Way South
Santa Ana, Calif. 92707
Telephone 714-979-8761

Gavin A. J. Trippe   President

Motor Racing Network
Div. of the International Speedway Corp.
P.O. Drawer S
Daytona Beach, Fla. 32015
Telephone 904-253-6712

Roger Bear   Exec. Producer

Helmet Safety Council
9107 Wilshire Blvd.
Suite 506
Beverly Hills, Calif. 90210
Telephone 213-272-3256

56

Snell Memorial Foundation
(Motorcycle Helmet Research and Testing)
c/o Sacramento County Hospital
2315 Stockton Blvd.
Sacramento, Calif. 95817
Telephone 916-454-2602

All-American Racers   Jerry Grant
(Development Work in Police Motorcycles)
2334 S. Broadway
Santa Ana, Calif. 92707
Telephone 714-540-1771

The Goodyear Tire & Rubber Co.   R. A. Shaffer   Asst. Field Mgr.
  Racing Division
1144 E. Market St.
Akron, Ohio 44316
Telephone 216-854-3078

Petersen Publishing Co.   Dick Day   Vice President
8490 Sunset Blvd.   Auto Publisher
Los Angeles, Calif. 90069
Telephone 213-657-5100

American Motorcycle Assoc.   Ed Youngblood   Executive
25 Collegeview Road   Director
Westerville, Ohio 43081
Telephone 614-891-2425

57

The Birmingham Small Arms
  Company Incorporated
Western Operations Center
2765 E. Huntington Drive
Duarte, Calif. 91010
Telephone 213-359-3221

E. W. Colman

Vice President

Norton Villiers Ltd.
Thruxton Race Circuit
Andover, Hampshire, England
Telephone Weyhill 2171

Frank Perris

Competitions
Manager

Field & Stream
P.O. Box 248
Magalia, Calif. 95954
Telephone 916-873-0900

Bob Behme

Vehicles Editor

58

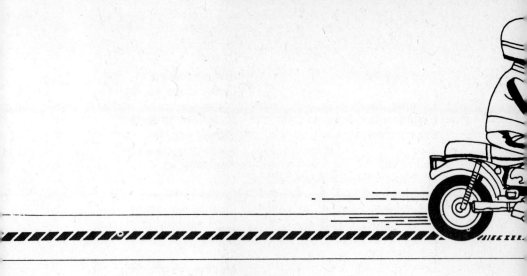

Index

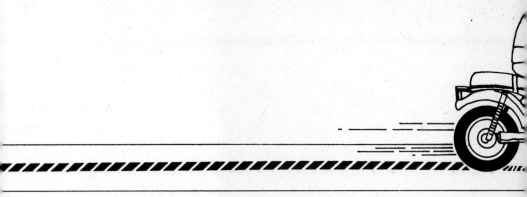

About the Author

Ross R. Olney is the author of more than sixty books on a wide variety of subjects. He has also written several hundred magazine articles, many of which have been on the subject of auto racing or other motor-oriented sports. His book entitled *Driving: How to Get a License and Keep it!* (A Concise Guide) was recently published by Franklin Watts.

Mr. Olney is a licensed underwater instructor for Los Angeles County, an accomplished photographer, and an avid camper. A native of Ohio, he now lives with his wife and three sons in Canoga Park, California.